The Window Song

The Window Song

LAURENCE DAVID
Photography by Cathy David

RESOURCE *Publications* • Eugene, Oregon

THE WINDOW SONG

Copyright © 2017 Laurence David. All rights reserved. Except for brief quotations in critical publications or reviews, no part of this book may be reproduced in any manner without prior written permission from the publisher. Write: Permissions, Wipf and Stock Publishers, 199 W. 8th Ave., Suite 3, Eugene, OR 97401.

Resource Publications
An Imprint of Wipf and Stock Publishers
199 W. 8th Ave., Suite 3
Eugene, OR 97401

www.wipfandstock.com

PAPERBACK ISBN: 978-1-5326-1912-0
HARDCOVER ISBN: 978-1-4982-4523-4
EBOOK ISBN: 978-1-4982-4522-7

Manufactured in the U.S.A.   JUNE 19, 2017

1

Without a spiritual seed
the body is like a bare tree.

The soul is a part of God
that blooms in every man's garden.

Prepare the soil,
but let God plant the seeds.

The spiritual seeds that come to fruition
stem from your meditation.

The seeds we take for granted
have yet to be planted.

The rose half-opened
hides the strongest scent.

Thunder claps its hands
and down come the rains.

A pure spirit hides behind
a wall of clear water.

Winding down a river road
nothing can stop the inevitable flood.

The raging river forms
a natural wall of sound.

Surrender to a river prayer
when its spirit pulls you under.

Ride out each new current
until all the ripples settle.

The soul stands alone in prayer,
like a pool of still water.

Imagine a riverbed
to put the flood to rest.

A fallen spirit is the fountain
that springs from the earth.

In time the sea will receive
the frozen spring.

Love is an ocean,
but we must drink from the fountain.

The sky and the sea
are part of the same blue dream.

A river prayer is realized
when love and nature coincide.

Heaven can make a body of water
spill over into the soul.

The Spirit leads you
to follow the course of nature.

Man's natural image reflects
back to the instinctual.

Instinct may lead you to a place
that's contrary to reason.

Instinct gives no thought
to good and evil.

A primitive spirit's only desire
is to conquer nature.

Man would be pure
if he could cure the heart of nature.

Nature possesses the hope
that what God has created will praise Him.

We can see nature
as our mirror.

Nature is screaming
for you to be silent.

Is there enough hidden truth
to be found anymore in nature?

2

The higher you climb the closer you get
to the impossibility of perfection.

The hope of perfection
still leaves you searching.

Getting lost in this world
is like being caught inside an open door.

There's no freedom in this place
without the constraints of time and space.

It may take years of traveling within yourself
before you arrive home at your true self.

How can you steer clear
of an internal drive?

Give way to the wheel
when it takes a turn for the better.

There's no telling which way the wheel's spinning
when it comes round to your turn.

Leave it to the rider
to put pressure on the wheel.

Struggling to get back on track
does not make you equal to the task.

Don't be last to join the race,
but only the first to escape.

The illusion of victory is concealed
by an underlying defeat.

Surrender now to failure
for the hope that comes after.

Success and failure are inverted
to fit into the world.

In his world success and failure
is how a man is measured.

Don't keep your pearl
hidden too long from the world.

A self-enclosed sanctuary
is certainly never safe.

Secrecy must protect its privacy.

The worse disconnection
is to lose your sole foundation.

Love with no spiritual bond
has no foundation to build from.

Some only worship the search for God,
instead of the source of their true desire.

Though we ask many questions of God,
He asks only one of us.

Ancient wisdom can never surrender
to the curse of the future.

Fortify what's left
of the established truth.

You can't hold the hand that's closed,
or ever own the open road.

Loss of control may only
strengthen your hold.

There's something to gain
from the pain of separation.

The ties that bind
wind up strangling the child.

A family is formed when
fragmented pieces coexist as one.

Romance has a way of bringing
fantasy down to reality.

Family life can be home
to a lot of heartache.

The hardest part of staying
is perfecting the art of waiting.

A small, silent decision
can have drastic repercussions.

3

The form that you're born into
can shape your entire life.

The spirit of man
is rejuvenated by youth.

A youthful spirit is a child
playing in a fountain.

The child in you needs to
play out his heart on the rocking horse.

Why say that wonder
is no cause for surrender?

Simplicity contains so much power
in such a small world.

It's no wonder the magical
can find no reason in this world.

Simplicity confounds a calculating mind.

How far we've fallen
from just the memory of innocence.

The sins of the father
pass through the hands of the child.

False innocence is
well acquainted with evil.

Innocence can be
ignorance of pain.

4

Faith will call forth
the child in a man.

Faith says, "Put your trust in me."

Let go with both hands
to see your world in flight.

We can drift through each day
by riding on faith.

Put your trust in the unbroken wheel
or you wind up going nowhere.

To be lost in these waters
is to drift alone with no faith.

To look towards the promise
is to sail blindly into the mist.

There's freedom to be found
in the hope of surrendering.

You may find the perfect plan
with only the thought of surrendering.

Hope allows reason
to play with the possibilities.

With faith there's still a chance
for the possibility of hope.

The loss of hope can kill
all possibility of escape.

The law acts as a thief
to steal your faith.

Who can fulfill their calling
before ever believing?

A soul on fire can bring
faith back from the ashes.

Faith that claims the reward
should be savored.

5

As soon as you resign yourself to life,
then the light of hope shines.

You need only envision a spark,
in light of all this darkness.

That light is somehow blessed
which shines from this darkness.

With no source of light the truth
would vanish with the darkness.

Center in to that source of light
that looks within.

Vision turns inward
to reflect the soul.

A true vision is seen
through the window of the soul.

See the Father
behind the child inside.

The other world you may be seeing
means more than the one you appear to be in.

Behind a man's shining eyes-
a sad, dark outlook.

The man who closed his eyes
is looking for someone to be his guide.

No apologies from the
man who won't see.

There's no light looking
through the world's eyes.

The blind eye must be looking
for signs where they don't appear.

A vision to the blind
tumbles blindly through the night.

Even the smallest shadow
can cloud your vision of the truth.

Vision must seem like a dream
before it can be revealed.

Winter light is a yearning for life.

The sky can hide
all but the memory of light.

Looking back reflects
a mirrored image of the past.

Looking back left
a cracked image behind the glass.

The purpose of this life is to leave behind
a light that shines forth.

An image is best served
for its spiritual message.

Outside every religion
is vision looking in.

The strongest light
emerges in afterglow.

6

There's no greater mystery
above the one that doesn't appear to be.

The mystery of creation is not knowing
what form its spirit will take.

Sometimes the mystery moves
in a circuitous way.

The Circle is a mystery
you can never complete.

The puzzle never fits the frame
till all the pieces fall into place.

You don't need complexity
to explain a mystery.

You may discover that reason
only shadows the mystery.

Reason may hope to lay claim
to what will remain unknown.

7

A man can only imagine,
who's only known the thoughts of a dream.

In the imagination you must
be a dreamer to be a believer.

At the heart of a dream
you may hear the beating from within.

Dreams that remain unseen
may lose their meaning.

Just altering the face of a dream
can never change your heart.

The purity of a dream is forever lost
when it falls to earth.

A shattered dream
leaves a heart of stone.

The dream has died
but you find you're still alive.

When dreams die young
a man grows old believing nothing.

The death of a dream
dissolves into memory.

When the hope of a dream dies
the struggle to believe survives.

In time we may long for the possibility
of a long forgotten dream.

A simple dream hopes
to be more than impossible.

Let the long forgotten dream be realized,
however long after its time.

Who could endure the pain
without the comfort of a dream?

When the Spirit awakes it marks
a return to peace for the dreamer.

The Spirit may stay the dream
that causes you to remain.

God's dream of acceptance
is our dream also.

What kind of man would exploit someone
by turning their dreams against them?

Take heed of the dream
consumed by its own desperate need.

Chasing a dream can drive you
away from your true self.

The dreamer hopes that he
can stay pure from the world.

An empty dream
has neither passion nor pain.

In a fallen world dreams of happiness
will always fall short.

We need to be floating free,
so that we can dream.

Don't disturb our peace
for anything but a dream.

8

True song is a true dream
spinning all on its own.

That lone voice crying out
will touch the heart in solitude.

No voice rings truer
than that of the pure singer.

A universal message comes through
with each true voice.

It's nothing to silence a voice
that's long been ignored.

It's useless to sing
into a silent wind.

It's hopeless to cry
into a dying wind.

One shrill note can
shatter your window song.

The song of a broken dream
can break your heart again.

Sometimes only the chimes
of solitude ring true.

Songs of freedom chime
from the bells that once rang true.

Art is pure when it can
capture the heart of nature.

In true art there's the endless
search for greater simplicity.

It takes a world of inspiration
to capsulate the truth into one small line.

A proverb is a tiny diamond
that never stops shining.

Creativity can be a continual
source of renewing energy.

Motion can force
the wheels of creativity.

When the ice starts to thaw,
inspiration begins to flow.

Don't try to unfurl
an artist's self-enclosed world.

There's not much left of the artist
who's been consumed by business.

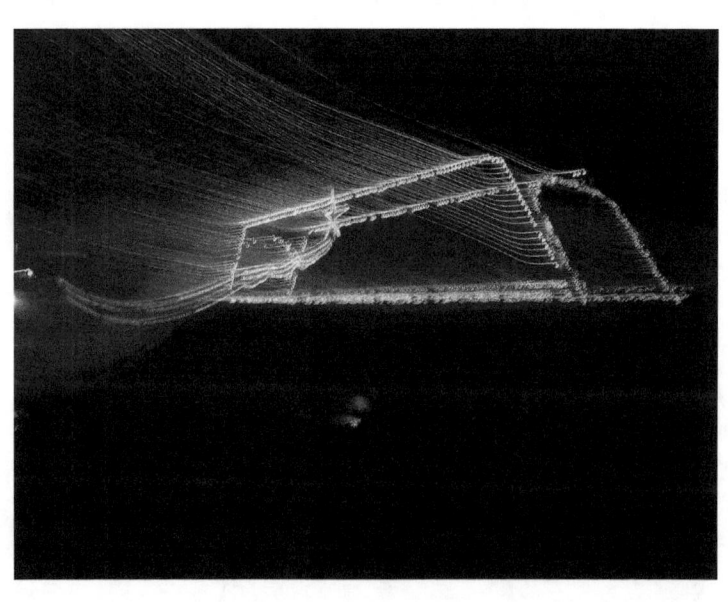

9

Some pay with passion
for the illusion of security.

Passion is vanquished
the same as every other fire.

Passion can kill,
or it can breathe life into the fire.

Why decry the passion
that screams from within?

Passion breathes fire
into the heart of darkness.

Passion breathes fire
into an empty wind.

Passion keeps the child
in the heart of a man.

Passion turns reason
into foolishness.

Passion is the fire
that ignites a dream.

Passion is tied
to the dream that takes flight.

Passion runs deep
for the life of a dream.

Passion runs free
from the spirit of man.

Passion rules the heart
when tears are consumed by fire.

Don't allow your passion
to rule your Spirit.

It's tragic if your passion
is the dream you can't attain.

Passion is desire
not easily quenched.

10

Fear is an anchor
that keeps you tied to the deep.

The human spirit will not
fly out of fear.

It's hopeless to try and stand on faith
with fear underneath.

Fear won't let your spirit
embrace its joy.

By surrendering to fear
you no longer rule your heart.

The heart cries out
within the confines of fear.

The child inside only appears
to hide your internal fears.

Worry is waiting behind
the shadow of a doubt.

There will be fear of the unknown
until the veil is lifted from the future.

Our future is never free from
the fear of what came before.

Fear of death
destroys what's left.

11

The heart bears witness of the truth
to the voice inside of you.

The heart is the source
of your one true dream.

A heart that's true
must embrace its purity.

The purest love flows
from the heart's blood.

The strongest love cuts through
to the deepest wound.

The heart embraces love
that reaches out with open arms.

We reach for a love that will
touch our hearts with open arms.

The heart remains unbroken
from a long standing love.

Love chances to risk it all
for an unbroken heart.

A heart that's failing
can never hope to win.

A broken heart and a contrite spirit
both know the source of defeat.

Because of a broken heart
the true self must hide in shame.

The heart that has no place
must beg for acceptance.

The heart cries out for peace
with nothing left to feel.

The heart of darkness is
cursed by its own blindness.

There's still a little evil left
in the darkest corners of the heart.

Hearts that are trapped are bound together
with no will to escape.

What captures the eye
may also rule the heart.

Hearts that lay claim to the promise
cannot be refused.

One thing the heart is sure about,
is one day the truth must come out.

The heart is full of memories
the mind has tried to bury.

While the heart races ahead,
the mind reaches back in its memory.

Heart and soul must always
return home to solitude.

Every heart believes in a place
where the soul will finally escape.

Cut from the source a soul will drift
until it's forever out of touch.

In any man the soul must
find expression and acceptance.

Through the window of the soul
the Spirit is carried home.

12

The Spirit carries on
for the soul that's carried off.

Like the wind, the Spirit drifts along,
waiting for someone to come.

The Spirit works despite
the laws of nature.

The Spirit is still able
to permeate the impenetrable.

It's the nature of the Spirit
that everything has its season.

There's no hidden future
to be feared in the Spirit.

The mind is full of worries
the Spirit dissolves into memories.

The Spirit compensates
for a soul's past mistakes.

Thank the Spirit for
the sake of the body.

Prayer brings your Spirit
deep into its own world.

In the Spirit is the only
open door to peace.

The Spirit cannot heal a wound
within the confines of religion.

If there's an answer,
the Spirit of Truth will reveal it.

The Spirit spins a dream that says
it may yet turn out your way.

A pure spirit in this world
is neither here nor there.

A pure spirit cannot be held too long,
or ever ignored.

A restless spirit blown out on the road
is left with nowhere else to go.

When the sky and the open road are clear,
then so is your spirit.

Through no fault of its own,
the spirit of man falls to flesh and bone.

In time the spirit of man
becomes a stranger to himself.

The spirit of man reaches out of the dark
to capture the human heart.

The spirit of man reaches up
for the final push towards heaven.

13

The natural tendency of the Spirit
is towards peace.

The Spirit lives
with the hope of peace.

After much traveling in the Spirit,
we finally arrive at a state of peace.

To the question of faith,
the Spirit answers with peace.

Put your soul to rest
with hope that it will know peace.

Peace is a bed for the soul.

It may take years of dreaming
to reach a peaceful sleep.

There's a moment of peace
when all the restless dreams cease.

Peace is an undying ember.

We hope to find the last remnants of peace
in the eye of the storm.

A place in the crowd
is a source for more chaos.

Our only chance for peace
is just inside our reach.

Stay anchored in peace
while all the chaos is swimming around you.

It's a false sense of peace
that draws you into those dark waters.

Peace that results from destruction
is a false peace.

Some would kill in the false hope
of achieving peace.

Destruction may force you
into a false peace.

Fighting for peace is a world
that's screaming for justice.

Beware of the destructive force
behind the battle for peace.

14

How easily a man's nature turns
from creation to destruction.

Those who justify war
have never felt the horror.

You can choose power
that will end the war.

When there's a confrontation of power,
when do we move to surrender?

Aggression destroys everything it can
to reach its end.

The explosion between love and hate
has left a ruin in its wake.

Hatred is a river that runs
as thick as blood.

It's reflex to hate
the cause of your rejection.

What is the source of the wound
that underlies your curse?

Satan rules the soul
when the hawk captures the dove.

Anger must not cross the line to violence.

Let your anger be the fire
that disperses like smoke.

Modern man fans the flame with vengeance.

The song of revenge
is no reason for celebration.

Has the storm begun to rage
before your anger could escape?

Don't let the storm disperse your anger
before it can escape in prayer.

Aggression is no longer the law of the land
once we're in the Kingdom of Heaven.

15

In a fallen world
freedom is the first to go down.

Since the fall there's been no escape
from this downward spiraling staircase.

There's no escape from this maze
for those who lead you astray.

The world is a boulder
that's leaning to tumble.

Everything in this world is a celebration
of the existence of imperfection.

Everything man has touched
has the stamp of imperfection.

Sin is a reflection
of the world of imperfection.

A lost soul tries
to find itself in sin.

There's no greater hell than
the one that's screaming from within.

The power of darkness
crawls deep into the night.

It's not courage that gives you
the power to surrender to evil.

Addiction is voluntary slavery.

Does the price of a thrill
buy more than your soul?

A sense of power
makes for the perfect liar.

A liar turns you into a fool
for believing him.

There's a false spirit behind
all the small hidden lies.

Is it pride or shame
that needs a lie to save face?

Darkness discovered your pride
long before the morning light.

The imagination has the power
to create a god in any image.

There's power when intelligence
and evil join forces.

Evil has no lack of imagination.

Our last chance for peace
came with the loss of justice.

In this world justice
is no measure of success.

For a just man the laws
of this world inspire contempt.

For you to condemn a man to hell
is the ultimate in self-righteousness.

God will show you a glimpse
of justice to keep you honest.

To hope against the world is to fight against the madness:
to pray against the world is to rave against the madness.

16

A wall of resistance stands against
everything we believe in.

A strong wind represents
the spirit of resistance.

Nature flies in the face of
everything that resists the wind.

Troubled waters could not
stem the tide of resistance.

The wall of indifference
keeps you retreating.

How does a man fall behind
with his back to the wind?

Faith in acceptance
to counter the law of resistance.

Fight through the false pride of defense.

Don't disturb the silence
between the lines of defense.

Have you found the freedom
to surrender what has you imprisoned?

Some choose to leave
before love turns to grief.

The enemy that's tugging
at your friend may win.

As with the color of dreams,
enemies may appear to be friends.

Envy works as a wedge between friends.

The only cure for the source of envy
is to let it be.

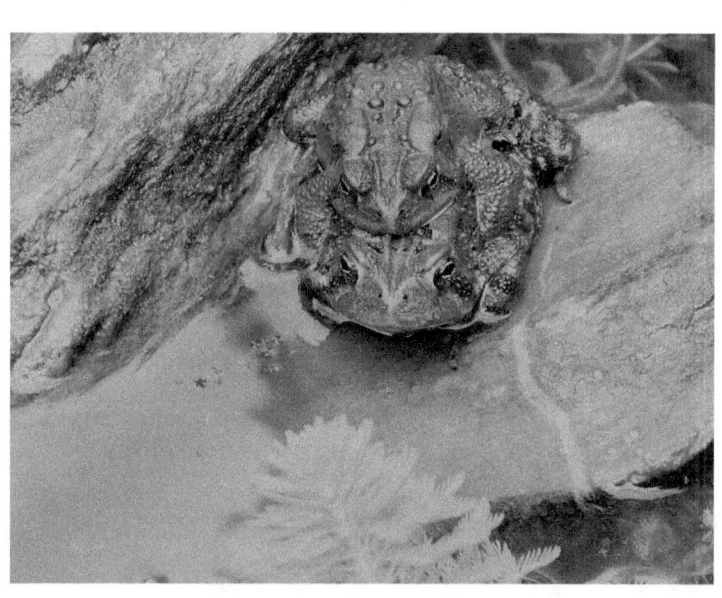

17

Everyone dreams of that brief moment
when youth and beauty dance together.

Beauty brings power
in the eyes of the world.

Youth and beauty play their
lovely game together.

Youth is full of daring.

Beauty marries wealth.

For beauty, her face is
the center of her attention.

Beauty and mystery combine to form
the missing piece of the puzzle.

Beauty is made into an idol
that truth calls a liar.

With Satan beauty is masked
by the horror beneath.

What chance has beauty
in the race against time?

The mark of aging
is a yearning for youth.

Fame doesn't mean
you found your fortune.

Fame causes a name to spread
beyond its common thread.

It's not God that
shines down on fame.

Only fools find meaning
in that circus surrounding the famous.

Fame is a mirrored image
turned inside out.

Fortune and fame cannot hide
the face of all shame.

18

The seduction of wealth is thinking you can walk
above all the worst in the world.

Pride stands before the mountain,
not knowing it will fall.

Pride stands tall atop the hill,
to capture those who never fall.

Pride will bring to the surface
all the foolishness in a man.

With enough praise, we start to think
our foolishness has significance.

Why does your success
make you full of yourself?

Blessings occur to win favor.

In the wrong hands a gift of the Spirit
can eliminate the need for the Spirit.

What good is a gift
for those who make it their god?

Greed makes sure you get
more than what you need.

Why say less is never better
when too much is not enough?

The street that's paved with gold
leads away from the open road.

The loss you most fear
is of what you hold most dear.

Changes occur to alter what appears.

Is it the master or the servant
that hides behind the guise of humiliation?

Pride pours shame on
the wounds of humiliation.

Pride was sent to
humble the oppressed.

There's no comfort for a wound
with no hope from a friend.

A heart in need
cannot embrace its poverty.

Don't hide your face in shame
behind a veil of humiliation.

You may appear empty-handed
to those unaware of what's in the heart.

Poverty puts you
in the role of the fool.

The fool looks down,
like a sad, but smiling clown.

The homeless man has nowhere
but his own world to retreat to.

The homeless man has no place
to hide but in obscurity.

The time of never is when
there's no hope for something better.

Why must poverty be
tied to ignorance?

Because they go hand in hand,
poverty and ignorance must do their dance.

If you can separate poverty from ignorance,
you may yet stop the dance.

Weakness seeks the same strength
that power corrupts.

19

Pain is released
into the hands of death.

Let go of the ghost
that's struggling to die.

A man is drawn into the fire
like a moth consumed by the flame.

The road that leads to death
goes the way of all flesh.

We find the final word
on the last stone uncovered.

Death demands silence in its wake.

The power of death
tears at the heart.

The place that death visits
is left behind in silence.

An empty body inherits the wind,
like a ruin.

Too much is left in the hands of death
to touch anybody's life.

The purpose of disease is to keep the mind
and the body embedded in the earth.

Will we die with our song unsung,
and our work just begun?

There's no good ending
without a true beginning.

Keep at least a spark alive
before the flame finally dies.

There's hope at the end of this future.

Love can reach beyond death
to breathe life back into the fire.

After continual failure there are
no remnants left of success.

After the sentence of defeat,
there's still the promise of victory.

Failure is not always
the banner for surrender.

20

Christ's humiliation was not appearing
to be who He really is.

He surrendered His body
to eradicate the face of death.

He bled so our bodies will not be sacrificed in vain:
He died so our Spirit will not be saved in vain.

The star of Bethlehem
foreshadowed the blood of Jerusalem.

It was no less a burden
when God took up the yoke of man.

Humility was blessed
for the sake of the oppressed.

Christ was champion
of His own shame.

One Word unspoken
will remain unbroken.

Through the Son the Father can
understand what's fragile and human.

There's no final end to the pain
unless Christ is the source of the healing.

www.ingramcontent.com/pod-product-compliance
Lightning Source LLC
LaVergne TN
LVHW051707080426
835511LV00017B/2776